D0469693

LONG LIVE THE KING!

by
Johnny Hart
&
Brant Parker

A FAWCETT GOLD MEDAL BOOK

Fawcett Publications, Inc., Greenwich, Connecticut.

1-26

Z-10

2-18

3-4

3-5

3-9

3-20

3-25

4-1

4-4

4-8

AMAZING!... JUGGLING **SIX** WINE BOTTLES WITHOUT A **GOOF**... HOW DOES HE **DO** IT ?

... THEY'RE FULL.

4-10

WIZ, WE NEED **RAIN** ... GET BUSY ON IT!

How to make rain.
(turn to page 46)

FLIP
FLIP
FLIP
FLIP
FLIP

4-13

5-1

5-11

5-13

5-19

5-21

6-12

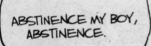

6·27

6-29

7-6

7-16

7-22

In the *Wizard of Id* Series

THE KING IS A FINK	13709-0	$1.25
THE PEASANTS ARE REVOLTING	13671-X	$1.25
REMEMBER THE GOLDEN RULE	13717-1	$1.25
THERE'S A FLY IN MY SWILL	1-3687-6	$1.25
THE WONDROUS WIZARD OF ID	1-3648-5	$1.25
THE WIZARD'S BACK	1-3654-X	$1.25
THE WIZARD OF ID—YIELD	1-3653-1	$1.25
THE WIZARD OF ID #8	1-3681-7	$1.25
LONG LIVE THE KING	1-3655-8	$1.25
WE'VE GOT TO STOP MEETING LIKE THIS	1-3633-7	$1.25
EVERY MAN IS INNOCENT UNTIL PROVEN BROKE	1-3650-7	$1.25